Fractions with Fish

By Maeve Sisk

GS
MATH

Please visit our website, www.garethstevens.com. For a free color catalog of all our high-quality books, call toll free 1-800-542-2595 or fax 1-877-542-2596.

Library of Congress Cataloging-in-Publication Data

Sisk, Maeve.
Fractions with fish / by Maeve Sisk.
  p. cm. — (Animal math)
Includes index.
ISBN 978-1-4339-9309-1 (pbk.)
ISBN 978-1-4339-9310-7 (6-pack)
ISBN 978-1-4339-9308-4 (library binding)
1. Fractions—Juvenile literature. 2. Fishes—Juvenile literature. I. Sisk, Maeve T. II. Title.
QA117.S594 2014
513.26—dc23

First Edition

Published in 2014 by
Gareth Stevens Publishing
111 East 14th Street, Suite 349
New York, NY 10003

Copyright © 2014 Gareth Stevens Publishing

Designer: Nicholas Domiano
Editor: Therese M. Shea

Photo credits: Cover, p. 1 Rich Carey/Shutterstock.com; pp. 3–24 (background texture) Natutik/Shutterstock.com; p. 5 Zoonar/Thinkstock.com; pp. 6, 8, 10, 16 iStockphoto/Thinkstock.com; pp. 7, 13, 17, 18 iStockphoto/Thinkstock.com; p. 9 stockpix4u/Shutterstock.com; p. 11 Hemera/Thinkstock.com; p. 14 falk/Shutterstock.com; pp. 15, 21 Comstock/Thinkstock.com; p. 19 © iStockphoto.com/mehmettorlak; p. 21 Katrina Brown/Shutterstock.com;

Printed in the United States of America

CPSIA compliance information: Batch #CS13GS: For further information contact Gareth Stevens, New York, New York at 1-800-542-2595.

Contents

Boldface words appear in the glossary.

Fish Schools

A fraction is part of a whole. We can learn about fractions with fish. Check your answers on page 22.

Many fish live in **schools**. A fraction of this school is red.

5

All Kinds of Fish

Some fish live in freshwater. Some fish live in salty ocean water.

We can put 2 fish into 2 sets. One fish is in each set. Each fish is ½ of the whole group.

Clownfish live in the ocean.

"Equal" means having the same amount. We can put 3 clownfish into 3 equal sets. Each fish is $\frac{1}{3}$ of the whole group.

This is a lionfish. It uses **poison** to kill other fish!

There are 4 lionfish. One out of 4 is in a box. That is the same as ¼.

11

These fish are called bigeyes. Can you tell why?

There are 6 bigeyes. Put them into 2 equal groups. How many are in each group?

?	?

Shark!

This is a great white shark. It has about 300 teeth!

Which group shows ¼ of the great white sharks in a box?

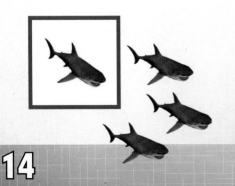

15

The whale shark is the largest fish.
It eats plants and small fish.

A whale shark sees 4 fish. It eats
2 fish. What fraction did it eat,
¼ or ½?

Fish at Home

Freshwater fish are good pets. There are about 100 kinds of goldfish!

There are 3 goldfish in a bowl. Then 1 goldfish jumps out. What fraction jumps out, $\frac{1}{3}$ or $\frac{1}{2}$?

19

Many people keep bettas as pets. Bettas are colorful.

There are 6 bettas. How many bettas are red? What fraction of the bettas is red?

21

Glossary

poison: something that causes illness or death

school: a group of fish

Answer Key

page 12: 3 bigeyes

page 14: group on left

page 16: $\frac{1}{2}$

page 18: $\frac{1}{3}$

page 20: 3 bettas, $\frac{3}{6}$ or $\frac{1}{2}$

For More Information

Books

Dowdy, Penny. *Fractions*. New York, NY: Crabtree Publishing, 2008.

Shaskan, Trisha Speed. *If You Were a Fraction*. Minneapolis, MN: Picture Window Books, 2009.

Stevens, Kathryn. *Fish*. Mankato, MN: Child's World, 2009.

Websites

Fish

animals.nationalgeographic.com/animals/fish/

Read about and see many photos of different kinds of fish.

Fractions

www.internet4classrooms.com/skill_builders/ fractions_math_first_1st_grade.htm

Find many links to fraction games.

Index